Congressional Research Service
Informing the legislative debate since 1914

Public Financing of Presidential Campaigns: Overview and Analysis

R. Sam Garrett
Specialist in American National Government

January 29, 2014

Congressional Research Service
7-5700
www.crs.gov
RL34534

Summary

The presidential public campaign financing program (the Presidential Election Campaign Fund [PECF]) is funded through "checkoff" designations on individual income tax returns. Choosing to participate (or not) in the checkoff does not affect one's tax liability or refund. Candidates who choose to participate in the program may receive taxpayer-funded matches of privately raised funds during primary campaigns, and grants during the general-election contest. Public funds also subsidize nominating conventions. The public financing system has remained largely unchanged since the 1970s. However, there is general agreement that, if the program is to be maintained, updates are necessary to provide greater financial resources and higher spending limits to participants. Some contend that the program should be curtailed or eliminated.

This report discusses current controversies and arguments for and against public financing of presidential campaigns, legislative history, elements of the program, taxpayer and candidate participation, financial status of the program, recent legislation, and analysis of various policy proposals. If Congress chooses to alter the program, consensus will be necessary in what has historically been a particularly complex and contentious area of campaign finance policy.

In recent Congresses, most legislative activity has concerned efforts to curtail the program. In the 113th Congress, the House has passed legislation (H.R. 2019) to eliminate funding for presidential nominating conventions. The Committee on House Administration has reported two related bills (H.R. 94; H.R. 95). Other bills that would eliminate convention financing include H.R. 260; H.R. 1724; H.R. 2857; and S. 118. Another bill, H.R. 270, would eliminate convention financing but modernize other parts of the presidential public financing program.

As this report discusses, various options, each with potential strengths and weaknesses, exist for revisiting the presidential public financing system. Two other CRS reports contain overviews of specific topics addressed in this report. These include CRS Report R41604, *Proposals to Eliminate Public Financing of Presidential Campaigns*, by R. Sam Garrett; and CRS Report RL34630, *Federal Funding of Presidential Nominating Conventions: Overview and Policy Options*, by R. Sam Garrett and Shawn Reese.

This report will be updated occasionally to reflect major developments.

Contents

Figures

Tables

Contacts

Recent Issues and Arguments in Brief

The principal justification behind presidential public financing has been to reduce the need for private money in politics.[1] Public financing proponents argue that the program has increased competition in presidential elections by permitting those without personal wealth or substantial private fundraising resources to seek the office.[2] Public financing therefore relieves candidates from at least some of the burdens of time-consuming private fundraising. Finally, public financing is attractive to some because it can encourage candidates to limit their campaign spending in exchange for public subsidies.

Nonetheless, even those who support the presidential public financing program generally agree that it needs to be updated.[3] Except for increasing the checkoff amount in 1993, Congress has essentially left the program unchanged since its enactment in 1971, and substantial expansion in 1974. Many of the concerns surrounding public financing highlight financial competitiveness among candidates. As this report discusses, publicly financed candidates must adhere to spending limits, unlike their privately financed opponents. Those limits, however, are increasingly regarded as too low to permit effective campaigning. Since 2000, some major candidates have chosen to forgo public financing during the primary campaign.

The 2008 campaign cycle was regarded as perhaps the final one in which the program, as it currently stands, would remain a viable option for the most competitive candidates. As one scholar noted, "By 2008, it was clear that the public financing system, with its relatively paltry spending limits, was a luxury no serious candidate could afford, at least in the primary season."[4] Nonetheless, and despite that sentiment, several candidates chose to participate in public financing during the 2008 election cycle. The Republican nominee, Senator John McCain, initially applied for public funds in the primary, but later withdrew from the system. Senator McCain did, however, receive public funds for the general election.[5] The Democratic nominee, Senator Barack Obama, announced in June 2008 that he would not participate in public financing for the general election; he also did not accept public funds during the primary.[6] Senator Obama was the first major-party nominee since the program's inception to decline public financing entirely.

---

[1] This report supersedes CRS Report RL32786, *The Presidential Election Campaign Fund and Tax Checkoff: Background and Current Issues*, by now-retired CRS Specialist Joseph E. Cantor. Parts of this report are adapted from the previous report.

[2] For an overview of arguments in favor of presidential public financing, see, for example, Campaign Finance Institute, Task Force on Financing Presidential Nominations, "So the Voters May Choose ... Reviving the Presidential Matching Fund System," April 2005, at http://www.cfinst.org/president/pdf/VotersChoose.pdf.

[3] See, for example, Robert D. Lenhard, "A $3 Vote for Competitive Elections," *Washington Post*, March 8, 2008, p. A15; Campaign Legal Center and Democracy 21, "Presidential Public Financing: Repairing the System," conference report, December 9, 2005, at http://www.campaignlegalcenter.org/attachments/1614.pdf; and Democracy 21, "Reform Groups Urge House Members to Co-Sponsor Legislation to Fix Presidential Public Financing System," press release, February 7, 2007, at http://www.democracy21.org/index.asp?Type=B_PR&SEC={91FCB139-CC82-4DDD-AE4E-3A81E6427C7F}&DE={92F0FA14-AED0-4153-A1F4-28645410CB25}.

[4] Richard L. Hasen, "Political Equality, the Internet, and Campaign Finance Regulation," *The Forum*, vol. 6, no. 1, art. 7; at http://www.bepress.com/forum/vol6/iss1/art7. This electronic journal is not paginated.

[5] Letter from Donald F. McGahn, II, chairman, Federal Election Commission, to Senator John McCain, September 5, 2008, at http://www.fec.gov/press/press2008/McCainLetterCert.pdf.

[6] Shailagh Murray, "Obama Opts Out of Public Financing," *Washington Post* online, June 19, 2008, at http://blog.washingtonpost.com/the-trail/2008/06/19/obama_opts_out_of_public_finan.html?hpid=topnews.

In 2012, no major candidate accepted public funds. Although the Democratic and Republican national conventions received a total of approximately $36.5 million in public funds, the three candidates who chose to participate received a total of approximately $1.4 million. President Obama again declined public funding, as did Republican nominee Mitt Romney.

Although much of the recent debate over public financing has focused on how to save the system, some suggest that Congress should end the program. For those who oppose presidential public financing, the declining taxpayer participation rate (discussed later in this report) provides evidence that the program lacks public support. Opponents also contend that the program has failed to improve competition.[7] Some also object in principle to government-funded campaign subsidies, question whether truly competitive candidates need public financing, or both.[8]

113th Congress Legislation

Eight bills introduced in the 113th Congress would affect public financing of presidential campaigns. These measures include H.R. 94, H.R. 95, H.R. 260, H.R. 270, H.R. 1724, H.R. 2019, H.R. 2857, and S. 118. Each bill except H.R. 270 is devoted to repealing all or part of the presidential public financing program. In December 2013, the House passed (295-103) H.R. 2019, which would terminate public financing of presidential nominating conventions.[9] The Committee on House Administration has reported two related bills, H.R. 94 and H.R. 95. The former would eliminate convention financing; the latter would eliminate the PECF entirely and transfer the balance to the general fund of the U.S. Treasury.[10]

Unlike bills that would repeal the presidential public financing system, a bill introduced by Representative Price (NC) would maintain the current system but alter the amounts available to, and restrictions on, participating candidates. The bill, H.R. 270, would also create a public financing program for congressional campaigns. The measure is generally similar to H.R. 6448, introduced during the 112th Congress.

Major provisions of H.R. 270 would remove candidate spending limits, which have previously been a hallmark of the presidential public financing program. Candidates also would not receive "rescue funds" to respond to opponents who raise or spend significant amounts—another major provision of some state programs and most recent congressional legislation designed to maintain the program. Instead, candidates could receive more public funds than they could currently, while continuing unlimited private fundraising. They would, however, have to agree to limit the amounts of contributions they accept. Overall, H.R. 270 appears to propose a publicly financed supplement to unlimited private fundraising, albeit private fundraising subject to smaller individual contribution limits.

In brief, major (but, by no means, all) provisions of *presidential* public financing elements of H.R. 270 include

---

[7] For an overview of arguments against presidential public financing, see, for example, John Samples, "The Failure of Taxpayer Financing of Presidential Campaigns," in John Samples, ed., *Welfare for Politicians? Taxpayer Financing of Campaigns* (Washington: Cato Institute, 2005), pp. 213-249; and Bradley A. Smith, *Unfree Speech: The Folly of Campaign Finance Reform* (Princeton: Princeton University Press, 2001), pp. 103-105.

[8] See, for example, John Samples, ed., *Welfare for Politicians?*.

[9] Roll call vote no. 632, Dec. 11, 2013.

[10] See H.Rept. 113-291 and H.Rept. 113-292, respectively.

- raising the checkoff designation to $20 for individuals and $40 for married couples filing jointly;

- eliminating spending limits on publicly financed candidates;

- eliminating public financing of conventions;

- providing *primary* candidates with up to $100 million in matching funds through a 500% federal match of contributions up to $250;

- raising the qualifying threshold for private fundraising by *primary* candidates from $5,000 in 20 states to $25,000 in 20 states;

- requiring *primary* and *general-election* candidates who choose to accept public funds to limit the private contributions they receive to 50% of the individual limit (compared with the higher limit for traditional private fundraising, $2,600 in 2014); and

- providing *general-election* candidates with up to $150 million in matching funds through a 500% federal match of contributions up to $250.

112th Congress Legislation

On January 20, 2011, Representative Cole introduced H.R. 359; that measure would have terminated public funding of presidential campaigns and nominating conventions by repealing the checkoff mechanism.[11] Amounts already designated to the PECF would have been returned to the Treasury. As noted previously, the House passed the bill (239-160) on January 26. The same day, Senator McConnell introduced a companion measure, S. 194. The House and Senate bills were virtually identical. Unlike the Senate bill, however, H.R. 359 would have specified that PECF amounts returned to the Treasury should be used specifically for deficit reduction.[12] H.R. 3463 (Harper) contained virtually identical language to that found in H.R. 359, although the former bill would have also eliminated the Election Assistance Commission (EAC).[13] H.R. 3463 passed the House (235-190) on December 1, 2011. Finally, Section 620 of H.R. 2434 (Emerson), the FY2012 Financial Services and General Government (FSGG) appropriations bill, would have prohibited spending appropriated funds to administer the presidential public financing program during the fiscal year.[14]

Unlike bills that would repeal the presidential public financing system, two bills introduced by Representative Price (NC) would have maintained the current system but altered the amounts available to, and restrictions on, participating candidates. One of those bills, H.R. 414, was devoted solely to presidential public financing. By contrast, H.R. 6448 would have restructured the presidential public financing program and created a public financing program for congressional campaigns.

---

[11] For a brief overview, see CRS Report R41604, *Proposals to Eliminate Public Financing of Presidential Campaigns*, by R. Sam Garrett.

[12] As noted previously, the deficit-reduction language was included in a House amendment.

[13] EAC issues are beyond the scope of this report. For additional discussion, see CRS Report RL32685, *Election Reform: The Help America Vote Act and Issues for Congress*, by Eric A. Fischer and Kevin J. Coleman.

[14] For additional discussion of the FSGG bill, see CRS Report R42008, *Financial Services and General Government: FY2012 Appropriations*, coordinated by Garrett Hatch.

Major provisions of H.R. 414 and Senate companion S. 3312 included

- raising the checkoff designation to $10 for individuals and $20 for married couples filing jointly;

- eliminating spending limits on publicly financed candidates;

- eliminating public financing of conventions;

- providing *primary* candidates with up to $100 million in matching funds through a 400% federal match of contributions up to $200;

- raising the qualifying threshold for private fundraising by *primary* candidates from $5,000 in 20 states to $25,000 in 20 states;

- requiring *primary* candidates who choose to accept public funds to limit the private contributions they receive to $1,000 (compared with the higher limit for traditional private fundraising, $2,400 in 2008); and

- decreasing *general election* grants to $50 million, but adding a matching fund component of up to $150 million (also a 400% federal match of contributions of $200 or less), for a total *general election* public financing allocation of up to $200 million.

The second bill, H.R. 6448, was generally similar to H.R. 270 from the 113th Congress (described above).

Brief Legislative History

Despite calls for publicly financed presidential campaigns early in the 20th Century, Congress did not actively consider the idea until the 1950s. In 1966, Congress first enacted legislation authorizing taxpayer support for presidential and vice-presidential candidates and political parties. However, legislation enacted the following year essentially terminated the original program before it took effect.[15]

The current presidential public financing system was established in the 1971 Revenue Act, which permitted individual taxpayers (except nonresident aliens) to designate $1 ($2 for married couples filing jointly) to the PECF.[16] Amounts in the PECF are diverted from the Treasury's general fund for use by qualified presidential candidates (or party nominating conventions). Although Congress enacted the program in 1971, due to objections from President Richard Nixon, the statute called for a delay in beginning checkoff designations.[17] Candidates did not begin receiving funds until the 1976 election cycle.

The Federal Election Campaign Act (FECA), enacted in 1971 and amended throughout the 1970s, expanded the scope of the public financing program and set various criteria for participation.[18] In particular, the 1974 FECA amendments extended public financing, originally reserved only for

---

[15] See 80 Stat. 1587 and 81 Stat. 57 respectively.

[16] On the presidential public financing portion of the Revenue Act, see 85 Stat. 573.

[17] 85 Stat. 574.

[18] FECA is 2 U.S.C. §431 *et seq.* Public financing requirements are discussed later in this report.

general-election candidates, to presidential primaries and nominating conventions. The 1974 amendments also established the FEC and charged the agency with certifying eligible candidates, authorizing payments from the PECF, and conducting audits related to public financing.

Despite relatively minor changes, the presidential public financing program has essentially remained unchanged since the 1974 FECA amendments.[19] Congress most recently altered the program in 1993, when it tripled the checkoff designation from $1 to $3 for individuals and from $2 to $6 for married couples filing jointly.[20] The 2002 Bipartisan Campaign Reform Act (BCRA), the most recent major enacted change to the nation's campaign finance laws, did not affect public financing.[21]

Buckley v. Valeo[22]

The U.S. Supreme Court addressed public financing in its landmark 1976 *Buckley v. Valeo* decision, which considered various constitutional challenges to FECA. The Court upheld spending limits associated with public financing because candidates voluntarily accept the limitations in exchange for receiving taxpayer support. Those who are not publicly financed candidates, may spend unlimited amounts, provided that their campaign funds come from lawful sources. Under *Buckley's* reasoning, spending of nonpublic campaign funds is generally considered protected political speech.

How Public Financing Works

Elements of the Program

The presidential public financing program provides funds for three phases of the campaign: (1) grants to nominating conventions; (2) matching funds for qualified primary candidates; and (3) grants for general-election nominees. Convention funding goes to the Democratic and Republican parties' (or qualifying third parties') convention committees; funding for the primary and general elections goes directly to qualifying candidates' campaigns.[23] Under federal law, convention funding receives priority, followed by general election grants and primary matching funds.[24] In other words, primary matching funds are distributed only if sufficient amounts remain after first providing convention grants and general-election grants. Prorated amounts may be distributed in

---

[19] P.L. 93-443; 88 Stat. 1263

[20] 26 U.S.C. §6096(a). On the increase, see P.L. 103-66; 107 Stat. 567-568.

[21] BCRA is P.L. 107-155; 116 Stat. 81. BCRA amended FECA. For additional historical discussion of the evolution of campaign finance policy, see CRS Report R41542, *The State of Campaign Finance Policy: Recent Developments and Issues for Congress*, by R. Sam Garrett.

[22] 424 U.S. 1 (1976). For additional discussion, see CRS Report RL30669, *The Constitutionality of Campaign Finance Regulation: Buckley v. Valeo and Its Supreme Court Progeny*, by L. Paige Whitaker.

[23] For additional discussion of convention funding, see CRS Report RL34630, *Federal Funding of Presidential Nominating Conventions: Overview and Policy Options*, by R. Sam Garrett and Shawn Reese.

[24] On prioritization of convention funding, see 26 U.S.C. §9008(a).

the event of shortfalls (insufficient balances in the fund), which were a regular concern when candidates actively participated in the program.[25]

The Role of Taxpayers

Taxpayers determine how much money is available for presidential public financing through a "checkoff" provision on individual federal tax returns, as shown in **Figure 1**, below. Checkoff designations are the only revenue source for the public financing program, even if the Treasury Secretary projects that the fund will become insolvent.[26] Under current law, Congress makes no appropriation to the PECF.

Figure 1. The Checkoff Designation on IRS Form 1040

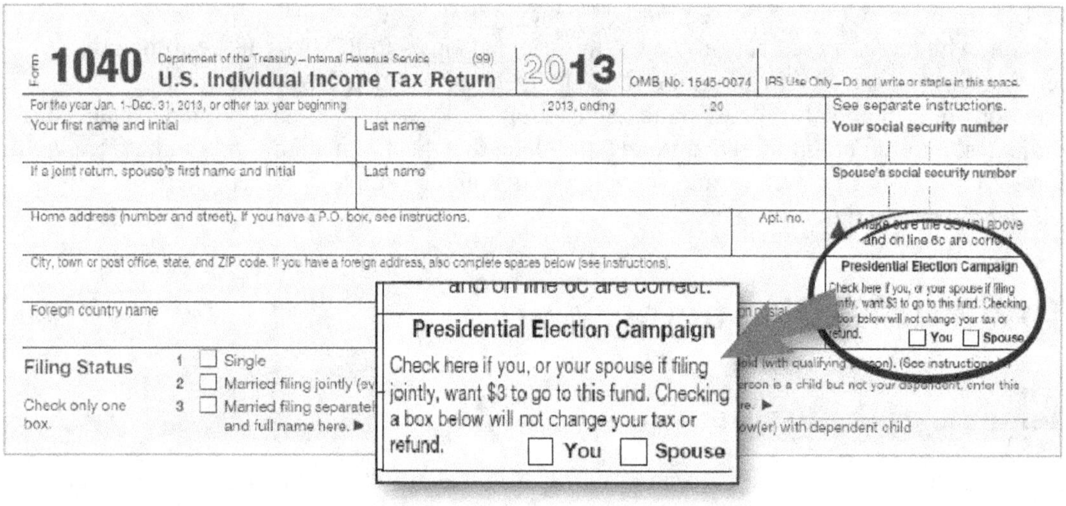

Source: CRS adaptation of IRS form 1040.

Individuals may choose to designate $3 of their tax liability to the PECF, a separate fund maintained by the U.S. Treasury solely to fund publicly financed presidential campaigns and nominating conventions.[27] Married couples filing jointly may designate a total of $6 to the fund, although, as the figure shows, separate response options are listed for each spouse.

Although taxpayers may believe that how they answer the checkoff question affects the amount of tax they owe or the refund they receive, "[d]esignating the allowed amount does not affect the amount of an individual's tax liability or tax refund; it simply directs the Treasury Department to

---

[25] Prorated funds are distributed under the so-called "shortfall rule," which requires the Treasury Secretary to "seek to achieve an equitable distribution" among competing members of the same political party. See 26 U.S.C. §9037(b). Therefore, in the event of a shortfall, those competing for matching funds receive approximately the same amounts. IRS regulations permit payments as soon as funds become available (rather than on the monthly basis specified in Title 26 of the U.S. Code) in the event of a shortfall. See Department of the Treasury, Internal Revenue Service, "Payments From the Presidential Primary Matching Payment Account," 73 *Federal Register* 8608, February 14, 2008; and Department of the Treasury, Internal Revenue Service, "Payments From the Presidential Primary Matching Payment Account," 73 *Federal Register* 67103, November 13, 2008.

[26] See, for example, 26 U.S.C. §9006(c).

[27] On the PECF, see 26 U.S.C. §9001 et seq.

---

allocate a specific amount from general revenues to the PECF."[28] In short, participating (or not) in the checkoff designation does not affect a taxpayer's liability or refund. Rather, it allows taxpayers to direct a small portion of the taxes they pay to the PECF instead of the Treasury's general fund.[29]

The Role of Federal Agencies

The Treasury Department and the FEC share responsibility for administering presidential public financing, although the FEC is the lead agency shaping program policy. Based on FEC certifications of candidate eligibility, the Treasury Secretary has responsibility for disbursing public funds. The Internal Revenue Service (IRS) administers the checkoff designations through individual tax returns.

Amounts Participants May Receive

Public financing benefits (amounts) are set by statute and vary by type of candidate and phase of the campaign.

- For their *nominating conventions*, each of the two major parties may qualify for grants of $4 million as adjusted for inflation (approximately $18.2 million each in 2012).[30] Based on their nominee's performance in the preceding election, *existing* third parties may qualify for lesser amounts. *New* third parties may receive limited public financing retroactively if they receive at least 5% of the popular vote in the general election, meaning that they are ineligible for funds until after the campaign concludes. (Funds received after the election could be used to pay remaining debts.)[31] A third party has received convention funds only once.[32]

- For the *general election*, the Democratic and Republican presidential nominees are eligible for $20 million grants, as adjusted for inflation (approximately $84.1

---

[28] Anthony Corrado, "Public Funding of Presidential Campaigns," in Anthony Corrado, Thomas E. Mann, Daniel R. Ortiz, and Trevor Potter, eds. *The New Campaign Finance Sourcebook* (Washington: Brookings Institution Press, 2005), p. 182.

[29] However, those who pay no taxes would not contribute to the program. See Department of the Treasury, Internal Revenue Service, "Payments From the Presidential Primary Matching Payment Account," p. 8608, which notes that "individuals whose income tax *liability* for the taxable year is $3 or more may designate $3 for the [PECF] on their tax returns." Emphasis added.

[30] Ibid., 26 U.S.C. §9008(b); 26 U.S.C. §9008(b)(2). On application procedures, see 11 C.F.R. 9008.3. The 2008 figures were aggregated by the author from $16,356,000 in Federal Election Commission, "FEC Approves Matching Funds for 2008 Candidates," press release, at http://www.fec.gov/press/press2007/20071207cert.shtml and $464,760 in an inflation-adjustment figure provided by Wanda Thomas, deputy assistant staff director for public financing, FEC (e-mail correspondence with author, April 9, 2008). Conventions also receive additional federal funding for security. On that topic, see CRS Report RL34630, *Federal Funding of Presidential Nominating Conventions: Overview and Policy Options*, by R. Sam Garrett and Shawn Reese. Although the FEC certified the 2008 Republican National Convention for the full $16.8 million allocation, the committee ultimately received $13.0 million. The convention ended early due to Hurricane Gustav.

[31] See, for example, 26 U.S.C. §9004(a)(3).

[32] The Reform Party received $2.5 million in 2000.

---

million each in 2008; had major-party nominees participated in 2012, the grants would have been $91.2 million).[33] Third parties may qualify for lesser amounts.

- Publicly financed *primary* candidates could spend up to $42 million in 2008 (plus approximately $14 million in fundraising, legal, and accounting costs, which are exempt from the base spending limit), but the amount of funds participants receive depends on their ability to secure government matching payments based on private fundraising. Limits in 2012 would have been $45.6 million, although no candidate approached that amount.[34] Participating candidates' individual contributions of up to $250 may be matched at a rate of 100% each. For example, a privately raised contribution of $200 would be matched for $200, bringing the candidate's total receipt of funds to $400. On the other hand, contributions of more than $250 are matched only for the first $250.[35] For example, a contribution of $1,000 would only be eligible for $250 in matching funds.[36] The primary matching fund program, which was designed to magnify small donations, applies only to individual contributions. PAC or party contributions are ineligible for matching payments. In 2012, only "minor" candidates received primary matching funds, which totaled approximately $1.4 million.

Qualifying for Public Financing

Candidates who wish to receive public funds must meet various qualifying criteria and agree to certain conditions designed to decrease the need for large contributions while also demonstrating the candidate's viability. To qualify for public financing in the primary, candidates must raise at least $100,000 in specific amounts and across various states. Specifically, candidates must raise at least $5,000, through individual contributions of no more than $250 each, in at least 20 states.[37]

If they choose to participate, the Democratic and Republican nominees are automatically eligible for public financing in the general election. Nominees of third parties (called "minor parties" in FECA) whose candidates earned at least 5% of the popular vote in the previous general election are eligible for lesser amounts.[38] However, third-party candidates rarely meet qualifying criteria, as discussed below.

---

[33] 2 U.S.C. §§441a(b)(1); 441a(c). The 2008 amount appears in Federal Election Commission, "FEC Approves Matching Funds for 2008 Candidates." Amounts for 2012 appear in Federal Election Commission, "Presidential Election Campaign Fund," press background brochure, http://fec.gov/press/bkgnd/fund.shtml.

[34] This amount appears in Federal Election Commission, "Presidential Election Campaign Fund," press background brochure, http://fec.gov/press/bkgnd/fund.shtml.

[35] The $250 cap applies to any single contribution or to small contributions from the same individual that aggregate more than $250. For example, a series of six $50 contributions (aggregating $300) would only be matched at $250.

[36] The base amount, without the inflation adjustment, is $10 million. On primary spending limits, see 2 U.S.C. §§441a(b)(1); 441a(c).

[37] 26 U.S.C. §§9033(b)(3); 9033(b)(4).

[38] The 5% threshold appears in the relevant definition applying to "minor parties." See 26 U.S.C. §9002(7). On eligibility for general-election payments, see 26 U.S.C. §§9004(a)(2); 9004(a)(3).

Conditions on Participation

Publicly funded *primary* candidates must adhere to overall and state-specific spending limits. The aggregate limit was approximately $42 million in 2008 (plus approximately $14 million in fundraising, legal, and accounting costs, which are exempt from the base spending limit). State-specific limits in 2008 ranged from $841,000 in sparsely populated states and territories, to approximately $18.3 million in California. These amounts were (and are) determined by a formula established in FECA (the greater of 16¢ multiplied by the voting-age population (VAP) of the state, or $200,000, as adjusted for inflation).[39] Publicly financed candidates in the *general* election must agree not to raise private funds for their campaigns. In exchange for the taxpayer-funded grant, their spending was limited to approximately $84.1 million in 2008; had major-party nominees participated in 2012, the grants would have been $91.2 million.[40] Finally, all publicly financed campaigns must: agree to various record-keeping requirements, submit to FEC audits, and limit spending from the candidate's personal funds to no more than $50,000.[41]

Participation Over Time

Participation in the public financing program can be considered on two fronts: (1) taxpayer participation; and (2) candidate participation in the program. This section discusses both.

Taxpayer Participation

Taxpayer participation has never been particularly strong. Even at the height of the program's popularity more than 30 years ago, less than one-third of taxpayers chose to support presidential public financing. As **Table 1** and **Figure 2** show, checkoff participation reached a high point in 1980, when 28.7% of filers designated funds for the PECF. With minor exceptions, participation has fallen steadily since that time. Fewer than 15% of taxpayers have made public financing designations every calendar year since 1993. Most recently, approximately 6% of taxpayers have participated in the checkoff. The "Analysis of Policy Options" section at the end of this report provides additional discussion.

Table 1. Checkoff Designations, Since 1973

Year[a]	Percentage of Returns Containing Designations	Total Amount Designated (current dollars in millions)	Total Amount Designated (constant [2013] dollars in millions)
1973	—	$2.4	$12.6
1974	—	$27.6	$130.4

---

[39] The base limit (before the inflation adjustment) is $10 million. See 2 U.S.C. §441a(b)1(A). For the 2008 limits, see Federal Election Commission, "Presidential Spending Limits for 2008," at http://www.fec.gov/pages/brochures/pubfund_limits_2008.shtml.

[40] The base limit (before the inflation adjustment) is $20 million. See 2 U.S.C. §441a(b)1(B). Data for 2012 appear in Federal Election Commission, "Presidential Election Campaign Fund," press background brochure, http://fec.gov/press/bkgnd/fund.shtml.

[41] 26 U.S.C. §§9003(a); 9033(a). On the $50,000 limit, see 26 U.S.C. §9006(d).

Year[a]	Percentage of Returns Containing Designations	Total Amount Designated (current dollars in millions)	Total Amount Designated (constant [2013] dollars in millions)
1975	—	$31.7	$137.3
1976	27.5%	$33.7	$138.0
1977	28.6%	$36.6	$140.7
1978	25.4%	$39.2	$140.1
1979	27.4%	$35.9	$115.2
1980	28.7%	$38.8	$109.7
1981	27.0%	$41.0	$105.1
1982	24.2%	$39.0	$94.1
1983	23.7%	$35.6	$83.3
1984	23.0%	$35.0	$78.5
1985	23.0%	$34.7	$75.1
1986	21.7%	$35.8	$76.1
1987	21.0%	$33.7	$69.1
1988	20.1%	$33.0	$65.0
1989	19.8%	$32.3	$60.7
1990	19.5%	$32.5	$57.9
1991	17.7%	$32.3	$55.2
1992	18.9%	$29.6	$49.1
1993[b]	14.5%	$27.6	$44.5
1994	13.0%	$71.3	$112.1
1995	12.9%	$67.9	$103.8
1996	12.6%	$66.9	$99.3
1997	12.5%	$66.3	$96.2
1998	12.5%	$63.3	$90.5
1999	11.8%	$61.1	$85.4
2000	11.5%	$60.7	$82.1
2001	11.0%	$59.3	$78.0
2002	11.3%	$62.0	$80.3
2003	10.1%	$59.4	$75.2
2004	9.2%	$55.7	$68.7
2005	9.1%	$53.3	$63.6
2006	10.9%	$51.0	$58.9
2007	8.3%[c]	$49.8	$56.0
2008	7.4%	$49.6	$53.7
2009	7.3%	$45.3	$49.2

Year[a]	Percentage of Returns Containing Designations	Total Amount Designated (current dollars in millions)	Total Amount Designated (constant [2013] dollars in millions)
2010	7.3%	$40.4	$43.2
2011	6.4%	$39.6	$41.0
2012	6.0%	$40.8	$41.4
Totals	—	$1751.7	$3,216.2

Source: Data for 1973-2006 calendar-year designations and checkoff amounts appear in Federal Election Commission, "Presidential Matching Fund Income Tax Check-Off Status, brochure, June 2008. CRS calculated all inflation-adjusted dollars based on the 2010 annual average. The checkoff percentage and designation (actual dollars) data for 2007 and later come from IRS data provided by the FEC, the IRS *Data Book*, or from the Congressional Budget Office.

a. Refers to calendar year for which funds were designated. Designations occur on tax forms submitted the following year (e.g., 2009 returns were filed in 2010).

b. As discussed elsewhere in this report, Congress increased the checkoff designation from $1 to $3 ($2 to $6 for married couples filing jointly) in 1993.

c. Checkoff percentage data since 2007 appear to be reported by fiscal year, whereas the pre-2007 data appear to be reported by calendar year. See also the table notes below.

d. Balance information for 2009 will be included in future updates to this report.

Notes: Some figures in the table differ slightly from source data due to rounding. The FEC source data notes that checkoff participation figures "are not available for the years 1973-1975," and that some 1973-1976 data cannot be verified. In general, historical data on public financing designations and amounts can vary by source and timing. This table generally relies on calendar-year data, but some data in the table are available only by fiscal year. It appears unlikely that the data reported in the table would vary substantially from one measure to another.

Figure 2. Taxpayer Participation in Public Financing Since 1976

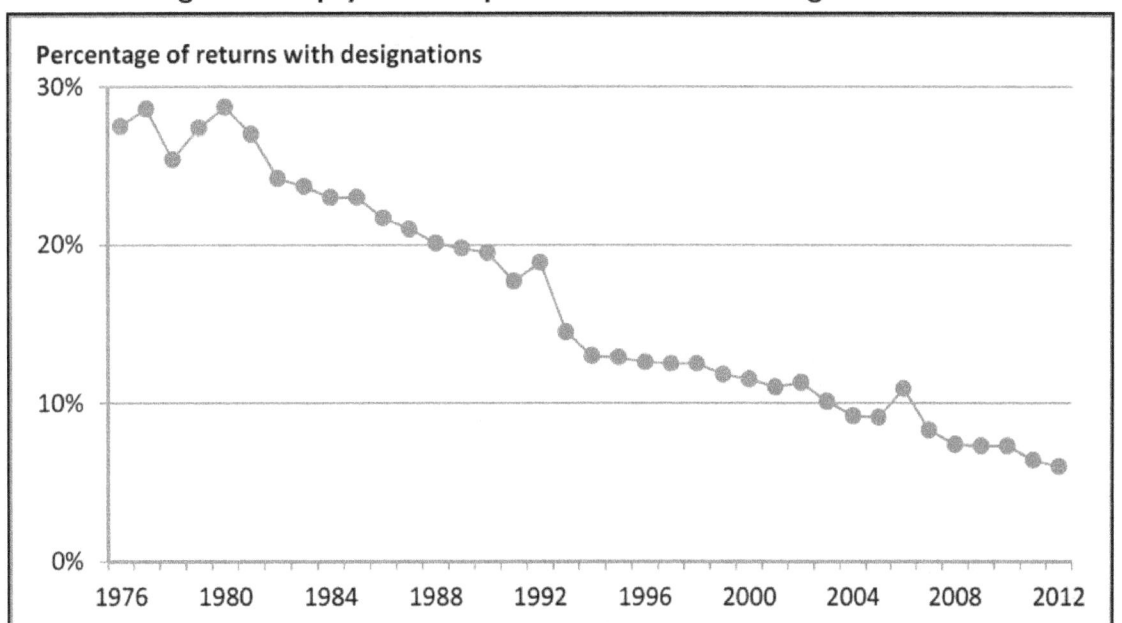

Source: CRS graph based on IRS data cited in Federal Election Commission, "Presidential Matching Fund Income Tax Check-Off Status," brochure, June 2008. Post-2008 data were provided separately to CRS by the FEC.

Candidate Participation

Almost every major presidential candidate since 1976 has participated in the public financing program. Exceptions were rare until the 2000 election cycle. Democrats and Republicans have participated in the public financing program on a roughly equal basis. Until 2008, every major-party nominee since 1976 had accepted public financing for the general election.

Historically, only a few wealthy, self-financed candidates declined to participate in public financing.[42] Beginning during the 2000 election cycle, however, some major candidates began to opt out of primary matching funds, apparently believing that bypassing required spending limits would be strategically advantageous. That year, George W. Bush participated in public financing during the general election but not during the primary. Then-candidate Bush was the first person elected president without having participated in public financing during both the primary and general phases of the campaign. In 2004, President Bush and Democratic nominee Senator John Kerry both declined public financing during the primary campaign.[43] Both accepted public funds for the general-election campaign.

Major candidates most recently participated in primary public financing in 2008. That year, the FEC certified eight candidates[44] as being eligible for matching funds in the 2008 primary campaign, as shown in **Table 2**. The Democratic and Republican parties were both certified to receive approximately $16.8 million each in convention grants. Because the Republican convention ended early due to Hurricane Gustav, however, the committee ultimately received approximately $13.0 million.[45] As noted previously, Senator Obama's campaign did not participate in public financing during the general election, unlike Senator McCain's campaign.

Table 2. Primary Matching Funds Certified by the FEC for the 2008 Election Cycle

Candidate	Amount Certified by FEC
Joseph Biden	$2,033,471.83
Christopher Dodd	$1,961,741.71
John Edwards	$12,882,877.42
Mike Gravel	$215,966.74
Duncan Hunter	$453,527.32

---

[42] Examples include Ross Perot (1992) and Steve Forbes (1996).

[43] Federal Election Commission, "FEC Approves Matching Funds for 2004 Presidential Candidates," final certifications, press release, April 1, 2005, at http://www.fec.gov/press/press2005/20050401cert html. See also Anthony Corrado, "Public Funding of Presidential Campaigns," p. 184.

[44] This number excludes the primary certification for Senator McCain's campaign. Senator McCain did not accept public funds.

[45] See Federal Election Commission, "FEC Approves Matching Funds for 2008 Candidates," press release, December 20, 2007, at http://www fec.gov/press/press2007/20071207cert.shtml for a base certification of $16,356,000. The FEC also certified an additional payment, to cover inflation, of $464,760. Information on the inflation adjustment comes from e-mail correspondence between the author and Wanda Thomas, deputy assistant staff director for public financing, FEC, April 9, 2008. The convention refunded the remaining amount of the 2008 allocation.

Candidate	Amount Certified by FEC
Dennis Kucinich	$1,070,521.05
Ralph Nader	$881,494.22
Thomas Tancredo	$2,228,900.85
Total	**$21,728,501.15**

Source: Individual certifications appear in Federal Election Commission, "FEC Approves Matching Funds for 2008 Candidates," press release, January 23, 2009, at http://www.fec.gov/press/press2009/20090123Matching.shtml; Federal Election Commission, CRS calculated the total. CRS also consulted Financial Management Service, Department of the Treasury, *Disbursements from the Presidential Election Campaign Fund and Related Payments*, February 28, 2009, report produced by the Credit Accounting Branch, provided to CRS by the FMS Office of Legislative and Public Affairs.

Notes: The table does not include funds initially certified for Senator McCain's campaign, which applied for primary matching funds but later withdrew from public financing during the primary campaign. The McCain campaign never received primary matching funds. The McCain campaign's status with respect to the public financing program during the primary is beyond the scope of this report. Other candidates who do not appear in the table either did not apply for public funds or did not qualify.

As noted previously, by 2012, candidate participation declined substantially. As shown in **Table 3** below, the "minor" candidates who chose to accept primary public funds received only about $1.4 million. No candidate received general-election funding. The two major parties both received convention grants.

Table 3. Primary Matching Funds Certified by the FEC for the 2012 Election Cycle

Candidate	Amount Certified by FEC
Charles E. "Buddy" Roemer	$351,961.10
Gary Earl Johnson	$632,016.80
Jill Stein	$372,130.44
Total	**$1,356,108.34**

Source: CRS calculated the total. CRS consulted Financial Management Service, Department of the Treasury, *Disbursements from the Presidential Election Campaign Fund and Related Payments*, December 2013, report produced by the Credit Accounting Branch, provided to CRS by the FMS Office of Legislative and Public Affairs.

The "Fringe" Candidate Question

Throughout the public financing program's history, some have raised concerns about whether those sometimes described as "fringe" candidates, who had no reasonable chance of winning, should be eligible to receive public funds. This report does not attempt to assess candidates' chances of success, and there is no clear definition of what might constitute a "fringe" candidate. It is clear, however, that the vast majority of public funds have benefitted Democratic and Republican candidates.[46] Specifically, third-party candidates, independents, and Lyndon LaRouche (who often ran as a Democrat) have collectively received about 4% of approximately

---

[46] In fairness, some of these candidates, too, might have also had little chance of success, even though they were affiliated with a major party. It should also be noted that candidate party affiliation occasionally varies by state, particularly for third-party candidates.

$1.3 billion provided to candidates overall.[47] Therefore, although those candidates who likely had the least chances of electoral success have received approximately $55 million, that amount is a small fraction of all funds distributed over the life of the program. A third-party nominating convention received public funds only once (the 2000 Reform Party convention; $2.5 million).

Financial Status of the Presidential Election Campaign Fund

The amount of money in the PECF depends on taxpayer designations and candidate use. As **Table 4** and **Figure 3** show, and as would be expected, the balance in the fund typically builds during off years and then drops sharply during presidential election years. For the past several years, as taxpayer designations have declined and campaigns have become more expensive, there has been widespread concern that the amount of money available in the fund—and spending limits for participants—were too low to make the program attractive to candidates.

Table 4. Presidential Election Campaign Fund Balances Since 1973

Calendar Year	Fund Balance (current dollars in millions)	Fund Balance (current [2013] dollars in millions)
1973	$2.4	$12.59
1974	$27.6	$130.42
1975	$59.6	$258.07
1976	$23.8	$97.44
1977	$60.9	$234.11
1978	$100.3	$358.37
1979	$135.2	$433.83
1980	$73.8	$208.64
1981	$114.4	$293.18
1982	$153.5	$370.56
1983	$177.3	$414.69
1984	$92.7	$207.85
1985	$125.9	$272.58
1986	$161.7	$343.70
1987	$177.9	$364.82

---

[47] These figures are based on CRS analysis of data provided by the Federal Election Commission, data in Federal Election Commission, *Report on the Presidential Public Funding Program* (FEC: April 1993), and data in FEC press releases. As noted previously, data on program totals sometimes vary over time and by source and are, therefore, subject to change.

Calendar Year	Fund Balance (current dollars in millions)	Fund Balance (current [2013] dollars in millions)
1988	$52.5	$103.38
1989	$82.9	$155.74
1990	$115.4	$205.69
1991	$127.1	$217.39
1992	$4.1	$6.81
1993	$30.8	$49.65
1994	$101.7	$159.86
1995	$146.9	$224.55
1996	$3.7	$5.49
1997	$69.9	$101.46
1998	$133.2	$190.37
1999	$165.5	$231.42
2000	$16.2	$21.92
2001	$75.0	$98.65
2002	$137.0	$177.40
2003	$167.3	$211.81
2004	$45.0	$55.50
2005	$98.0	$116.90
2006	$144.5	$166.98
2007	$166.3	$186.84
2008	$109.3	$118.26
2009	$152.1	$165.16
2010	$194.5	$207.79
2011	$199.1	$206.20
2012	$236.4	$239.86
2013	$271.6	$271.60

Source: Federal Election Commission, "Presidential Matching Fund Income Tax Check-Off Status," brochure, March 2009; CRS analysis of Financial Management Service, U.S. Treasury Department, data (post-2008). CRS calculated inflation-adjusted dollars.

Note: Figures in the table are rounded.

Figure 3. Presidential Election Campaign Fund Balances Since 1973

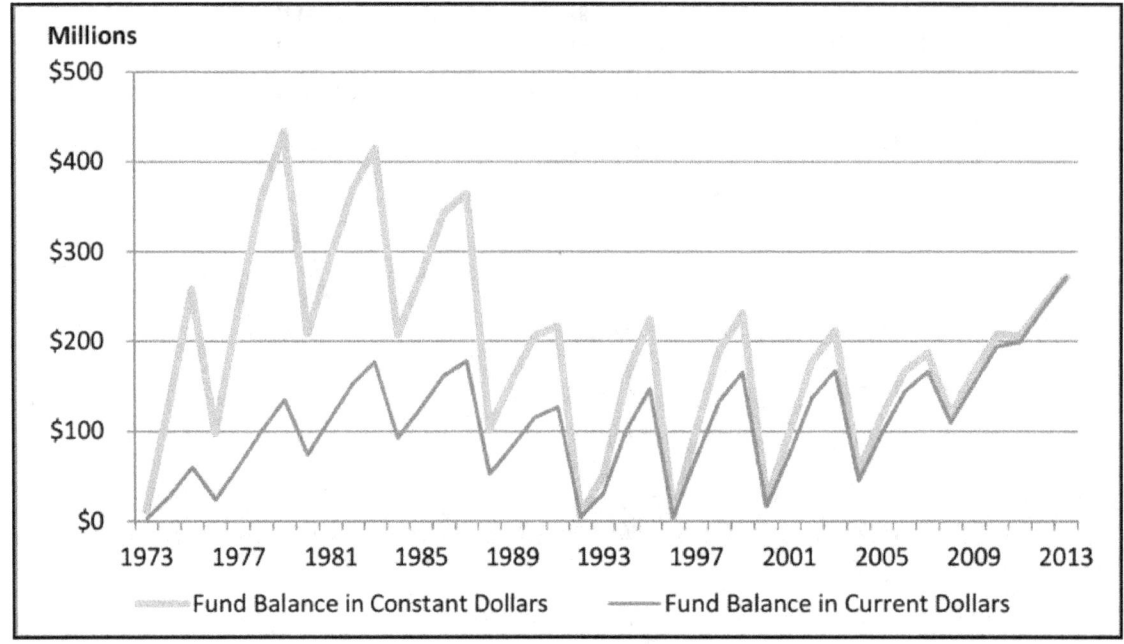

Source: CRS graph based on IRS data cited in Federal Election Commission, "Presidential Matching Fund Income Tax Check-Off Status," brochure, May 2007; post-2008 data provided separately by the FEC.

In an effort to avoid a projected shortfall in the PECF, in 1993 Congress increased the checkoff amount from $1 (or $2 for married couples filing jointly) to $3 (or $6). That change took effect for 1993 tax returns. Increasing the checkoff amount did infuse additional money into the PECF, but the fund has nonetheless struggled with shortfalls for primary matching funds. Additional discussion appears below.

Although fund balances were sufficient to pay the convention grants and general-election grants, shortfalls in primary matching funds occurred in 1996 and 2000.[48] A shortfall also occurred briefly in 2004, but major shortfalls were avoided, as eventual nominees George W. Bush and John Kerry, among others, declined to participate in public financing during the primary.[49] Shortfalls also occurred in the spring of 2008.[50] The larger issue during 2008, however, was the FEC's inability to certify matching-fund payments after the agency lost its policymaking quorum. Eligible candidates received matching funds after the quorum was restored. In the absence of broad candidate participation in 2012, shortfalls did not occur.

---

[48] For additional discussion, see Anthony Corrado, "Public Funding of Presidential Campaigns," pp. 183-184.

[49] Federal Election Commission, "FEC Approves Matching Funds for 2004 Presidential Candidates." See also Anthony Corrado, "Public Funding of Presidential Campaigns," p. 184. Information on the brief 2004 shortfall (which occurred between February and March of 2004) was provided by Wanda Thomas, deputy assistant staff director for public financing, FEC (e-mail correspondence with author, May 21, 2008). When shortfalls occur, candidates sometimes use certifications of their eligibility for public financing to secure private bank loans, which are subsequently repaid with public funds.

[50] Federal Election Commission, "FEC Approves Matching Funds for 2004 Presidential Candidates."

Analysis of Policy Options for Maintaining Public Financing

Various policy options exist for updating the public financing system. Some of those options are contained in recent legislation. Others discussed below present alternatives for addressing concerns surrounding presidential public financing, but are not components of recent legislation. The following sections discuss possibilities for increasing the amount of money available in the PECF and options for increasing the program's attractiveness to candidates. Taxpayer participation is also discussed. None of the policy options discussed in this report and elsewhere is likely to be considered in isolation, as the public financing program has always contained a combination of benefits and requirements.

Providing the Presidential Election Campaign Fund with More Money

As noted previously, the chief concern surrounding presidential public financing is the amount of money available to candidates. Shortfalls in recent elections have delayed matching-fund payments during primaries—a critical time for candidates to establish their viability and recognition among the electorate. General-election subsidies are also a concern, although generally not viewed as pressing as primary funds. Regardless of the phase of the election, a higher balance in the PECF could facilitate higher spending by candidates, provided that Congress raised spending limits.

Increasing the Checkoff Amount

Several recent reform proposals have proposed increasing the checkoff amount (such as from $3 for individuals to $10, or from $6 to $20 for married couples filing jointly). Although it is unclear precisely how an increased checkoff amount would affect the PECF, the one previous increase in the checkoff amount did not result in greater taxpayer participation in public financing. Rather, the checkoff rate fell by almost one-quarter (23.3%), from 18.9% in 1992 to 14.5% in 1993. As **Figure 4** shows, that 4.4 percentage-point decline was the largest calendar-year change in taxpayer participation in the program's history. Participation stabilized beginning in 1994.

Figure 4. Annual Percentage Change in Checkoff Designations

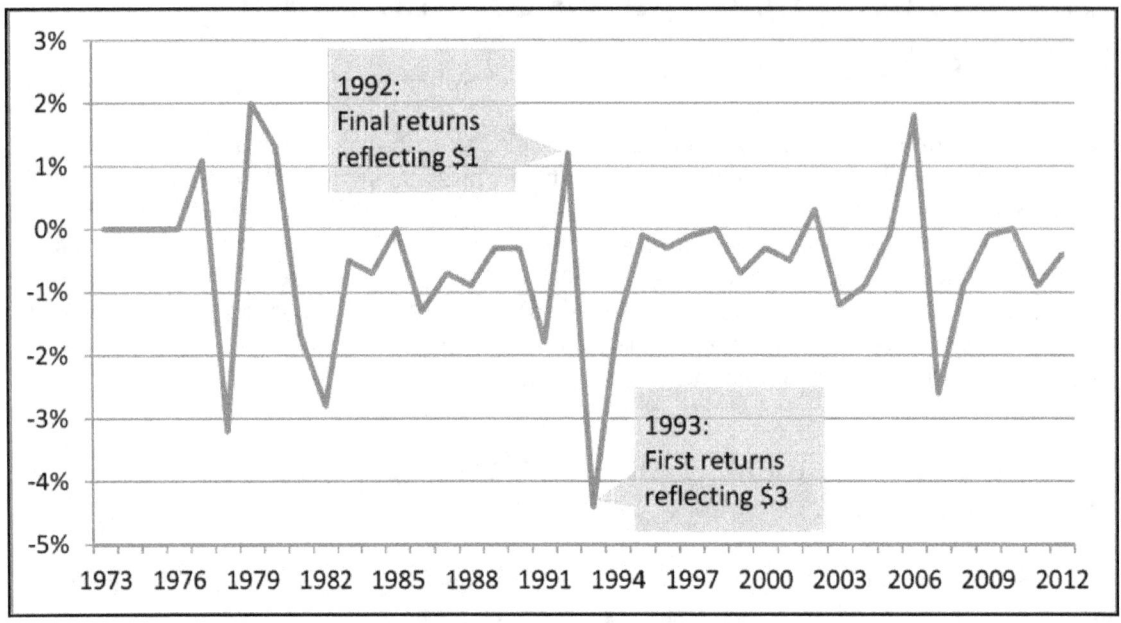

Source: CRS calculations of annual percentage change based on IRS data cited in Federal Election Commission, "Presidential Matching Fund Income Tax Check-Off Status," brochure, March 2009; post-2007 IRS data provided separately by the FEC.

Note: Checkoff percentage data since 2007 appear to be reported by fiscal year, whereas the pre-2007 data appear to be reported by calendar year.

Even with the decline in participation, increasing the checkoff amount did substantially bolster the fund balance (as shown in **Table 4** and **Figure 3**). The fund balance grew from approximately $4.1 million in 1992 (the final year of the $1 checkoff) to more than $30.8 million in 1993 (the first year of the $3 checkoff). Decreases in the fund balance are to be expected during election years (when most disbursements are made, thereby depleting much of the balance). However, the percent increase in the fund balance between 1992 and 1993 was far more than in the increase in the post-election years that preceded the checkoff increase (1977, 1981, 1985, and 1989). The median percent increase in the fund balance between those years and those that preceded them was 56.5%, compared with an increase of more than 650% between 1992 and 1993.[51] Even with that infusion of funds, and as is typical, the fund balance decreased sharply during the 1996 election cycle.

Overall, the 1993 change suggests that, if taxpayers respond as they did when Congress last raised the checkoff amount, the participation rate will fall if Congress raises the amount again. For example, a decline from the 2010 rate (7.3%) commensurate with the 4.4-point percentage drop in 1993 suggests that fewer than 3% of taxpayers (2.9%) would make designations to the PECF if the checkoff amount is increased. However, the designations that do occur, because of the higher dollar amounts, could nonetheless increase the amount of money in the PECF. It should also be noted that frequently proposed public education campaigns could either encourage or discourage participation.

---

[51] CRS calculated annual percentage change rates based on the FEC data cited in **Table 1**.

Changing the Qualifying Requirements to Limit Candidate Access to Funds

Rather than providing more money to the PECF, or in addition to doing so, Congress could choose to make it more difficult for candidates to qualify for public financing, therefore reserving funds for the most competitive candidates. Recent proposals have maintained a 20-state threshold, although the matching-fund amount would have decreased from $250 to $200. Legislation proposing to maintain the system would have required even greater fundraising requirements.

Any increase in fundraising prerequisites could make it harder for some candidates who have recently met the primary qualifying criteria to do so again. As shown in **Table 2**, the FEC certified only two candidates (Mike Gravel and Duncan Hunter) for matching funds in amounts less than $500,000 in 2008—the most recent period of substantial candidate participation. In the entire 2004 cycle, only one candidate (Alfred C. Sharpton) was certified for less than $500,000.[52] This suggests that increasing the qualifying threshold to $500,000 would not have had a great effect on the number of publicly financed candidates during the current and immediate past presidential election cycles, assuming that those candidates could have met the higher state-by-state fundraising thresholds. Raising the qualifying threshold to $500,000 also would not prevent any candidates from receiving public funds, if those candidates were able to meet the qualifying criteria. (Indeed, candidates who could meet the new criteria would receive more matching funds than they do currently.) A $25,000 per-state threshold, however, would have decreased the number of publicly financed primary candidates by half.

On the one hand, increasing qualifying criteria could decrease competition by shutting some candidates out of the process. On the other hand, the historical data suggest that serious contenders would be required to raise substantial sums throughout the nation anyway. In addition, preserving PECF funds through tougher qualifying requirements might provide additional resources for other elements of the public financing program.

Of course, Congress could consider other options to increase qualifying criteria beyond those envisioned in the current system or the legislation introduced recently. This assumes, however, that Congress wishes to limit the number of candidates who may receive public funds (to preserve money in the fund or for other reasons).

Reconsidering Funding Priorities

As noted previously, public funds are currently disbursed in the following priority: (1) convention grants; (2) general-election grants; and (3) primary matching funds. Prioritization of the convention grants has been criticized recently because these events are heavily subsidized by local host committees.[53] Some observers have contended that conventions also benefit from "soft money" (funds not regulated under FECA) that is otherwise banned in federal elections.[54]

---

[52] Federal Election Commission, "FEC Approves Matching Funds for 2004 Presidential Candidates."

[53] For an overview, see Anthony Corrado, "Public Funding of Presidential Campaigns," pp. 190-193.

[54] As noted previously, for additional discussion of convention financing, see CRS Report RL34630, *Federal Funding of Presidential Nominating Conventions: Overview and Policy Options*, by R. Sam Garrett and Shawn Reese. See also Steve Weissman and Ruth Hassan, "The $100 Million Exemption: Soft Money and the 2004 National Party Conventions," Campaign Finance Institute, July 2004, at http://www.cfinst.org/books_reports/pdf/full_partyconventions.pdf; and Campaign Finance Institute, "Inside Fundraising for the 2008 Party Conventions: Party Surrogates Gather Soft Money While Federal Regulators Turn a Blind Eye," n.d. [released June 2008], at (continued...)

If Congress believes that funding candidates should be the top priority in the public financing program, de-prioritizing convention funding could be an attractive option. Doing so could help avoid future shortfalls in primary matching funds by preserving money in the PECF that would currently go to conventions first. Nonetheless, shortfalls might then shift to general-election grants or convention grants (unless they were eliminated entirely).

More generally, Congress could also consider eliminating one or more segments of the public financing program. For example, if Congress felt that convention funding were no longer necessary, these subsidies could be eliminated entirely, as several recent bills have proposed. However, those concerned about the influence of private money, particularly soft money, in convention financing could object to conventions that are completely dependent upon private funds. In addition, given recent concerns about the viability of primary public financing, Congress could choose to eliminate matching funds and shift remaining amounts to the general election, convention grants, or both. These options could facilitate maintaining public financing in some form, and even bolster remaining portions of the program, without allocating new funds.

Other Revenue Sources

Current law requires that support for the program be limited to checkoff designations. Congress might also consider allowing taxpayers to contribute to the PECF in ways beyond the checkoff mechanism. Currently, taxpayers are not permitted to determine *how much* they wish to designate toward the presidential public financing program. Rather, they may only indicate *whether* they wish to designate the fixed amount displayed on the 1040 form. Instead, Congress could permit additional taxpayer donations to the fund, allow taxpayers to specify a designation amount, or expand the number of designation choices.[55] If taxpayers chose to make larger contributions than the $3 amount, revenues in the fund could increase. They could also decrease if taxpayers chose to make smaller designations than the current $3 rate.

Congressional Appropriations

Congress has structured the public financing program such that checkoff designations have been solely responsible for the fund's resources. If it chose to do so, however, Congress could appropriate some or all funds necessary to cover public financing needs. Most recent bills that propose to retain the system would permit appropriations. Under such legislation, however, would have had to repay those amounts, with interest, to the Treasury.[56]

Congressional appropriations could have the advantage of supplementing or replacing declining checkoff designations. If regular and sufficient appropriations could be secured, the financial stability of the public financing program might also be more predictable than is the case today. However, some Members could find appropriations objectionable. Appropriations are also subject to being reduced or eliminated. In short, the PECF does not currently benefit from appropriations, but it also is not dependent upon the annual appropriations process.

(...continued)

http://www.cfinst.org/books_reports/conventions/2008Conventions_Rpt1.pdf.

[55] Caps would be necessary, however, to prevent taxpayers from designating their entire tax liability for the PECF.

[56] Both Treasury funds and PECF funds are generated by tax revenues, meaning that one form of public funds would be used to repay another.

Making Public Financing More Attractive to Candidates

If candidates are to be convinced to accept public financing, they must be persuaded that the program's benefits outweigh its constraints. This calculation often depends on opponents' behavior, particularly whether they, too, are expected to accept public financing. When two opposing candidates choose to participate, even low spending limits or benefits are likely to be sufficient because both sides are equipped with the same financial resources and face the same constraints. If, on the other hand, candidates believe that they can fare better outside the system— or that their opponents are likely to opt out—participation is less likely. That scenario seems to have discouraged participation during the primaries in recent elections.

Some recent bills have proposed to dramatically increase publicly financed candidates' resources. However, public financing cannot control for all spending or fundraising that occurs in campaigns. Whether during the primary or general campaigns, candidates may be dissuaded from participating if they fear inadequate resources to respond not only to opponents, but also to opposing political action committees (PACs), 501(c) organizations, and other outside groups, some of which are arguably not regulated by campaign finance law. In the absence of a constitutional amendment restricting the political speech of these and other organizations, curtailing campaign spending—except voluntarily—is unlikely.

To summarize, increased benefits and spending limits are likely to be attractive to candidates, especially if both opponents participate. Even if candidate spending and resources are equal, however, publicly financed candidates could continue to face opposition spending from outside groups. Nonetheless, the proposed benefits and higher spending limits would provide publicly financed candidates with more resources than they would receive today.

Reconsidering Matching Funds and the Role of "Small" Donors

The question of "small donors" (generally defined as those giving less than $200) is related to recent proposals to increase the match for primary contributions. Increasing the match rate from the current 100% to 400% or 500% (as proposed in recent legislation) could increase the effect of small contributions. An increased match could also provide substantially greater resources to publicly financed candidates. This approach assumes that sufficient funds would be available in the PECF to cover the additional match.

Congress could also renew the focus on small contributions by permitting publicly financed campaigns to spend larger (or unlimited) amounts of funds raised through small contributions. This approach might or might not include matching funds. The effect could be to encourage candidates to focus their efforts on small contributions, while still providing government assistance for some campaign needs.

Focusing on small contributions would not necessarily contain campaign costs (another program goal), particularly for those candidates who were able to raise and spend virtually unlimited amounts. In fact, if spending limits were eliminated, public financing could become an additional, but potentially unnecessary, funding source for those already able to raise substantial private funds—even if they do so in small amounts.

Taxpayer Awareness of, and Participation in, Public Financing

There is little current information about how well taxpayers understand the public financing program.[57] FEC focus groups conducted nationwide in 1989 found that "citizens may not know why the public funding program was implemented or how it works. The [FEC research] also revealed, however, that taxpayers would like to know more."[58] In response, the FEC conducted an educational campaign in 1991 and 1992 that featured public-service announcements and media appearances by commissioners.[59] Taxpayer participation has nonetheless generally declined, especially in 1993 when Congress increased the checkoff designation amount.

In opinion polling, support for public financing (at various levels) fluctuates with question wording.[60] Although respondents tend to favor limiting the influence of private money in politics, they often react negatively to references to taxpayer funds or government support for campaigns. It is possible, therefore, that Americans support an alternative to *private* campaign financing as we know it, but nonetheless object to subsidizing campaigns through tax dollars, even though the checkoff designation does not change one's tax liability. Without updated research on how Americans feel about public financing and the checkoff, it is unclear whether the low participation rate is due to a lack of knowledge, objection to the program, or other factors. It is also unclear whether more taxpayers could be persuaded to make checkoff designations, and, if so, how.

Issues Regarding Tax-Preparation Software

One possible explanation for the low checkoff rate is the popularity of tax-preparation software. Some such software has been criticized for setting "no" as a default response to the checkoff question.[61] Most recent proposals to retain public financing would require the Secretary of the Treasury to issue regulations requiring that tax-preparation software not automatically accept or decline public financing designations. It is unclear what effects this requirement could have on the checkoff rate, although voluntary changes in the past appear to have had little effect.

In November 2005, H&R Block and Intuit, major vendors of tax-preparation software, reportedly agreed to requests from then-FEC commissioners Michael Toner and Scott Thomas and the Campaign Finance Institute to revise some software to not automatically select "yes" or "no"

---

[57] See, for example, Campaign Legal Center and Democracy 21, *Presidential Public Financing: Repairing the System*, conference report, December 9, 2005, at http://www.campaignlegalcenter.org/attachments/1614.pdf, p. 9. A CRS search of scholarly literature also confirmed the point.

[58] Federal Election Commission, *Report on the Presidential Public Funding Program* (FEC: April 1993), p. 75. An HTML version of the report is available at http://www fec.gov/info/pfund htm.

[59] Ibid. See Appendix 5 of that report for scripts of the public-service announcements.

[60] See, for example, CRS Report RL33814, *Public Financing of Congressional Campaigns: Overview and Analysis*, by R. Sam Garrett; and Stephen R. Weissman and Ruth A. Hassan, "Public Opinion Polls Concerning Public Financing of Federal Elections 1972-2000: A Critical Analysis and Proposed Future Directions" (Washington: Campaign Finance Institute, 2005), pp. 2-3, at http://www.cfinst.org/president/pdf/PublicFunding_Surveys.pdf.

[61] For additional discussion, see Campaign Finance Institute, "Leading Tax Software Firms Alter Their Presidential Fund Check Off Questions to Promote Fair, Informed Choices," press release, November 10, 2005, at http://www.cfinst.org/pr/prRelease.aspx?ReleaseID=6.

options in response to checkoff question, and to revise instructions to more accurately reflect IRS descriptions of the program.[62]

IRS data do not clearly address the effects of those changes, but the changes appear to have had little, if any, effect on the overall checkoff rate. As **Table 1** and **Figure 2** show, the checkoff rate fell slightly in 2005 compared with 2004 (from 9.2% to 9.1% respectively), but rose to 10.9% in 2006. It is possible that the increase between 2005 and 2006 was a result of the software changes, but it is impossible to know for certain with currently available data. Even if the software did foster changes between 2005 and 2006, the checkoff rate fell again in 2007 and after. IRS data do not isolate returns filed with particular commercial software, nor do they contain information about taxpayer knowledge or intent with respect to commercial software. Therefore, it is ultimately unclear what effect the software changes may have had, but they do not appear to have reversed the trend of declining taxpayer participation.

Analysis of Policy Options for Curtailing or Eliminating Public Financing

For those who are either philosophically opposed to public financing or who view the system as unnecessary, curtailing or repealing public financing could be desirable. Whether Congress chose to pursue those approaches or others, repealing or curtailing public financing could be a straightforward matter of time-limiting or striking the relevant sections of law, as opposed to considering various options and amending relevant law to change the program.

The preceding section on reconsidering funding priorities explains that repealing convention funding could preserve remaining amounts for primary matching funds and general-election grants. This option could also provide a financial boost to the PECF overall without allocating additional funds to the program. In 2012, convention grants accounted for approximately $36.5 million of the PECF's obligations. That same amount, if not obligated for conventions, could reduce the threat of shortfalls for matching funds or, if necessary in the future, general-election grants. On the other hand, those concerned about the role of private funds in convention financing could object to repealing public funds.

For those who object to public financing, repealing the program could provide a revenue source for other purposes. As of this writing, approximately $271 million is available in the PECF. Repealing the program would also remove taxpayer funding from presidential elections, a role that some lawmakers and others believe private contributions should fulfill. On the other hand, repealing public financing completely would leave presidential candidates entirely beholden either to self-financing or to private contributions. Even strong candidates may have difficulty raising enough funds to be competitive or may be uncomfortable with the notion that their candidacies are beholden to donors.

For those who believe that candidates should be able to financially support their own campaigns or garner private contributions to do so, ending public financing would likely be acceptable. However, for those who believe that private contributions or personal wealth should not automatically include or exclude otherwise qualified presidential candidates, public financing

---

[62] Ibid.

remains an important resource. In addition, if public financing and its required spending limits were no longer options, the pace of private campaign fundraising, and unlimited spending, are likely to increase, as candidates are constantly on guard for the next election and potentially high-spending opponents.

Concluding Comments

Warnings about the public financing system's demise are not unique to the present day. Even at its peak, the taxpayer-participation rate has never exceeded 29%. Although fund balances were sufficient to meet candidate needs throughout the late-1970s and 1980s, by the early 1990s the system began to show strain. Tripling the checkoff amount in 1993 provided a significant financial boost, although checkoff designations have generally continued to decline. Even with the larger checkoff amount, shortfalls have occurred at least briefly during the primary matching-funds phase of the program since the 1996 election cycle. Overall, almost from the beginning, the program has faced obstacles, even as most presidential candidates have participated in public financing.

The 2008 campaign cycle did, however, show evidence of unique challenges to the system. Although several candidates chose to participate in public financing during the primaries, those candidates who continued to actively pursue their parties' nominations into the spring and summer of 2008 chose to opt out of primary public financing. Some candidates, in just a few months (or less), raised more through private contributions than the entire primary spending limit for publicly financed candidates. By 2012, no major candidate chose to participate.

Some major candidates could still choose to participate in public financing, but the threat of major candidates *not* participating is likely to make the current program less viable in the future, as candidates will potentially feel increasingly compelled to forgo the system to be competitive. The current system also does not provide additional resources to counter spending from outside groups, such as PACs and 501(c) organizations. The rise of "super PACs" devoted to particular candidates may also provide additional financial resources—although these funds typically may not be coordinated with candidates.[63] For some observers, these challenges and a possible resurgence in small donors suggest that public financing is unnecessary and should either be allowed to fade away or should be repealed outright. Others, however, contend that the program has provided vital assistance to high-quality candidates who are nonetheless unable to raise large sums of private contributions, or who choose not to do so.

Any policy choice that maintains the public financing system with expanded benefits is likely to be expensive. On the other hand, proponents argue that the increased cost is a worthy investment in presidential campaigns. Precise costs would depend on funding sources, program elements, and candidate participation.

If Congress chooses to maintain presidential public financing, it could be useful to consider what goals that system should pursue and how. The existing model of the checkoff designations appears to be either poorly understood by the taxpayers, unpopular with the taxpayers, or both. If that model is to be maintained, a commitment to educational outreach, and perhaps basic research

---

[63] For additional discussion, see CRS Report R42042, *Super PACs in Federal Elections: Overview and Issues for Congress*, by R. Sam Garrett.

about public opinion of, and knowledge about, presidential public financing could be useful. Perhaps more fundamentally, if Congress chooses to reform the program, doing so will require consensus among lawmakers about one of the most complex and contentious areas of campaign finance policy.

Author Contact Information

R. Sam Garrett
Specialist in American National Government
rgarrett@crs.loc.gov, 7-6443